Future Inventor

Future Snowboarder

Future Dancer

D1302389

Future Musician

Future Chef

Future Artist

Future Engineer

To my girls, Jess and Cat, who are both AWESOME! – C.H.

For Eloise Matthews – A.P.

First edition for the United States and Canada published in 2018 by Barron's Educational Series, Inc.

First published in 2018 by Scholastic Children's Books

Text copyright © Caryl Hart, 2018

Illustration copyright © Ali Pye, 2018

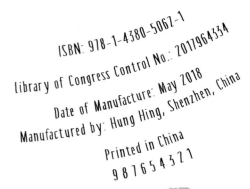

ISBN: 978-1-4380-5062-1

Library of Congress Control No.: 2017964334

Date of Manufacture: May 2018
Manufactured by: Hung Hing, Shenzhen, China

Printed in China

9 8 7 6 5 4 3 2 1

All rights reserved.
No part of this publication may be reproduced or distributed in any form or by any means without the written permission of the copyright owner.

All inquiries should be addressed to:
Barron's Educational Series, Inc.
250 Wireless Boulevard
Hauppauge, New York 11788
www.barronseduc.com

CARYL HART

# GIRLS
## Can Do
## ANYTHING

ALI PYE

**BARRON'S**

Girls come in all different colors and sizes.

They delight and amaze us.
They're full of surprises.

Girls can do **anything** they want to do. And if **YOU** are a girl...

...you can do these things too!

Girls can have **long hair**
or **short hair** in spikes.

Girls can ride **scooters**
and **skateboards** and **bikes.**

Girls can wear **pants** or **board shorts** or **dresses**.

Girls can be **neat** ...

... or make **wonderful** messes.

Girls can be **scruffy** or muddy and fragrant.

Like people on TV, girls can look **radiant**.

All girls are **different** ...

...but **one** thing is true—

there's **NO** other girl on the planet like **YOU!**

Girls can play
basketball, soccer, or catch,
or score lots of goals
in an ice hockey match.

Girls can climb mountains
and other high places.

And **win golden medals**
in all sorts of races.

Girls are **amazing.**
So shout it out loud—

"I'm a GIRL!
I'm FANTASTIC!
I'm strong, brave, and proud!"

Some girls like numbers and some prefer writing.

Some girls find science or music exciting.

Some girls are skillful
with pom-poms and glue.

But all girls are
**brilliant,**
and that includes
**you!**

Now here is a secret the whole world should know—
girls get MORE awesome the older they grow.

Some help
protect tigers...

...or heal
people's pets.

Some learn to be zookeepers, farmers, or vets.

Girls can **drive trucks** to
haul heavy loads,

or build fancy houses, or dig up the roads.

Girls can be **brave**
like this firefighter here,
**rescuing people** when danger is near.

Girls can be **gentle,**

and girls can be **rough.**

You can **count** on a girl when the going gets tough.

Girls are **amazing.** So shout it out loud—

"I'm a GIRL! I'm FANTASTIC! I'm strong, brave, and proud!"

MARIE CURIE

EMMANUELLE
CHARPENTIER

CLARA BARTON

ALEXA CANADY

Now, how many girls have **invented** a way
to make people´s lives a bit better each day?

ELIZABETH BLACKWELL

ROSALIND FRANKLIN

FLORENCE NIGHTINGALE

HUALAN CHEN

They've **discovered** the causes of coughs, spots, and sneezes
and learned how to treat many nasty diseases.

A girl can explore a hot jungly place,

or float in a rocket ship way out in space.

A girl can find clues

to help **solve**

tricky crimes.

Or **speak out for others**
at difficult times.

When a girl is determined, she **always** succeeds.
Her **courage** and **strength** are what everyone needs.

Girls are amazing.
So shout it out loud—
"I'm a GIRL! I'm FANTASTIC!

I'm strong, brave, and proud!"

And the girl I love best
in the whole world is YOU.
Dream BIG, special girl.
Tell me, what will YOU do?

**Claudia Gordon—Lawyer**
First deaf African American female attorney in the US

**Maryam Mirzakhani —Mathematician**
First female and Iranian winner of the Fields Medal, 2014

**Arunima Sinha—Mountaineer**
First female amputee to climb Mount Everest

**Marin Alsop—Conductor**
First female chief conductor of the Vienna Radio Symphony Orchestra

**Serena Williams—Tennis Player**
Tennis champion and icon

**Jane Goodall—Primatologist**
Ethologist, anthropologist, and UN Messenger of Peace

**Nicola Adams—Boxer**
First female and openly LGBTQ person to win a boxing gold medal at the Olympics

**Sue Wimpenny—Builder**
Builder and CEO